I0055985

Jeff Bowick & Dwayne Henriksen

OPTIONS TRADING CRASH COURSE: ADVANCED OPTIONS TRADING TOOLS

A simple but practical guide to operating in the market in a clever and conscious way

© **Copyright 2021 - All rights reserved.**

This document is geared towards providing exact and reliable information in regard to the topic and issue covered.

- From a Declaration of Principles which was accepted and approved equally by a Committee of the American Bar Association and a Committee of Publishers and Associations.

In no way is it legal to reproduce, duplicate, or transmit any part of this document in either electronic means or in printed format. All rights reserved.

The information provided herein is stated to be truthful and consistent, in that any liability, in terms of inattention or otherwise, by any usage or abuse of any policies, processes, or directions contained within is the solitary and utter responsibility of the recipient reader. Under no circumstances will any legal responsibility or blame be held against the publisher for any reparation, damages, or monetary loss due to the information herein, either directly or indirectly.

Respective authors own all copyrights not held by the publisher.

The information herein is offered for informational purposes solely and is universal as so. The presentation of the information is without contract or any type of guarantee assurance.

The trademarks that are used are without any consent, and the publication of the trademark is without permission or backing by the trademark owner. All trademarks and brands within this book are for clarifying purposes only and are owned by the owners themselves, not affiliated with this document.

Table of Contents

INTRODUCTION

In this book you will find some good trading tips and indispensable rules to not make mistakes. You will find concepts that it is good to keep in mind, among which there are important ones coming from Warren Buffett, one of the greatest investors in history, if not the greatest.

To put into practice the advice you will find, you can start with a trading platform that allows you to practice with a demo account, without making deposits and therefore without risk.

The first piece of advice is based on a famous quote by Warren Buffet: "To be successful in the stock market you only need to be afraid when others are greedy and be greedy when others are afraid".

In fact, three are the main enemies of the trader/investor's action on the market: "greed", "fear" and "hope".

When one is greedy, one wants to get everywhere, and tries to arrive on all price fluctuations, while the second one does not allow us to "be there" at the right moment.

Fear often turns into panic and makes us sell at the minimums; greed often pushes us to buy back near the maximums. Hope makes traders act against their true interests: the inexperienced and the deluded hope when they should be afraid and fear when they should hope.

Another famous Warren Buffett quote introduces another important concept: "There must be something perverse about the human character, because he likes to make easy things difficult."

To be successful in options trading you have to make difficult things easy, not the opposite, and above all, you should not look for complexity everywhere. Complex does not mean profitable, quite the contrary.

One of the most common mistakes in trading is not to follow the market trend or to follow it when it is too late and everyone has already taken advantage of it. Have you ever heard this slogan: "trend is your friend!"? That's right, the trend is your friend.

Trend analysis is the most valuable thing for those who want to trade online on financial markets and get economic results. From here comes another advice: follow the trend because the trend is your friend.

Another piece of advice gleaned from the usual Warren Buffett's experience is aimed at long term investors: don't fear uncertainty. Here is what the famous investor said: "Uncertainty is actually the friend of the long-term investor".

In the long term, the market always "digests" the storms that hit the financial markets. So sometimes it makes sense to buy at low prices during the storms and then sell at high prices as soon as the calm arrives.

Another very interesting slogan is: the market discounts everything. This indicates that all the fundamentals known by traders (and also by trading insiders) are already incorporated in the stock prices.

But surely the most famous slogan of the master and the most useful is: "The first rule is not to lose money, the second rule is never to forget the first rule". The goal of investment and speculation is the preservation of capital.

Now that we have clarified our ideas a bit and understood which guidelines we should follow, what about diving deeper and discovering specifically which are the real tricks and secrets to operate at best in the market?

CHAPTER 1 POINTS OF INTEREST FOR OPTIONS TRADING

In stock option trading, there is more than just buying and selling contracts.

If you're thinking about going into trading or dabbling in it right now, here are some common issues that arise every day in trading stock options.

And these aren't merely questions of theory. At some point during your stock options trading career, each one represents a decision you will have to make. Answer wrong, and the odds are good that you will find yourself out of the money more times than you want to be.

Give a quick quiz to yourself. Do you know the best answer to the Top 12 Questions about Trading Options?

• When are you getting your premium? And does your premium receipt mean that you are in the money?"

- Should your broker charge you interest when you write Puts? If you write Puts?

- What are the Naked Puts and Covered Calls difference?

- Is there a reason why you should write Covered Calls instead of Naked Puts?

- When should you write Secured Puts for Cash? And when do you ever have to write to them?

- When selling Covered Calls, how do you factor in Time Decay?

- What's the best stock options strategy for Naked Puts hedging?

- Should you ever close the Early Naked Put?

- What's the best stock options strategy for stop-loss trading?

- Does re-investing dividends make sense?

- How does your cost basis affect reinvested dividends?

- What type of trading strategy includes the sale of Covered Puts?

All of the questions have answers that are simple but significant. And what makes the difference between an options trading expert and someone who is simply throwing money into the market and hoping for the best is knowing those answers.

Several traders love to use more sophisticated options strategies in their trading, but the fairest trade for the market situation is the simple call options trade. To increase your likelihood of profiting from call option trading, follow the steps below.

1.   Determine that the price is going up for the underlying instrument. Call options trading is a directional strategy. This means that you have to choose the market direction, and the market should move up to profit. There are many different ways in which upward market movement can be anticipated. Some individuals react to good market news, and some use basic data such as increasing profits per share, increasing revenue, increasing dividend yield, etc. Some use chart patterns, such as the double bottom, reverse head, shoulder, ascending triangle, and upside price breakout, to indicate upward market

movement. Some utilize other systems, such as Elliot waves, and systems that use price pattern combinations and other indicators.

2.   Determine the price movement's target. A target price for the activity should also be indicated by the system that you use to show an upward price movement.

3.   To move to your target price, anticipate the time for the underlying price. How long do you expect the cost of the underlying tools to move to the target price? To determine the expiry of the call options you wish to trade, this is essential.

4.   Look at the string of options. To see the prices and other relevant data, bring out the options chains. Nowadays, chains of real-time options are easily accessible through the internet. To get this information, you can also call your broker.

5.   Narrow down to the date of exchange and expiry. If you trade online, determine the business to be submitted for your order. Based on the time you expect the price to change, choose a suitable expiration date. Usually, unless

you use a trading system that trades options near their expiry, you would like to buy call options with an expiry that is slightly longer than the expected time. This fact is to decrease the effect of time decay. This fact is very significant because time decay can lead to a loss of value for your call options.

6.   For several strike rates of the same expiry, compare the Delta, Gamma, Vega, and Theta. After you have narrowed down your options chain to the specific exchange and specific expiration date, you look at the Greeks. Ideally, you would like to have high Delta, high Gamma, low Vega, and low Theta. When the underlying instrument's price moves up, High Delta and High Gamma can give you a more significant and faster profit. Low Vega is very critical when you're buying options. Low Vega implies cheaper options, and you make profits even if the underlying price does not move when Vega increases. The low volatility and quiet market are associated with Low Vega. And Low Theta means that due to time decay, the call option causes smaller losses. You can choose out-of-the-money call options if you are a longer-term trader. Such alternatives have a

smaller delta but are cheaper. If you are a shorter-term trader, because they can give you faster and higher profits due to higher Delta and Gamma, you would prefer at-the-money or in-the-money call options.

7.   Based on your target price, assess your risk versus rewards. You can also use a risk profile to assist you in making the assessment. Use this formula to calculate the breakeven point: breakeven = call strike + call premium

8.   Look at the interest and volume that is open. In an active market, it is better to trade so that you can easily purchase and sell. Another reason is that on the bid/ask spread, and you don't lose a lot.

9.   Select the best option for the call with the highest profit probability.

10.   Determine the exit point and prevent loss. Before you place in your trade, make sure you have your profit taking points and stop-loss points in place. Do this so that your emotions do not take over your decision-making after you put in your trade.

11.   Place your trade-in. Call your broker online or key in your trade.

12.   Watch the price movement of the underlying instrument and the price response of the option.

13.   Close your stance. If you have made a profit, close your position by either selling your purchased call options or exercising the call option and selling the shares. It is usually better to sell the call options if there is some time remaining before expiry because there is still time value. If you have made a loss by selling the call options, close your position.

Credit Diffusion Strategy

If you have been option trading for a bit, you may have come across a credit spread strategy for one option. Somehow, credit spread appears to be a popular strategy because it has been touted as a means for traders to consistently make money from the market by taking advantage of time decay.

At this point, I think it is crucial to align our understanding of the credit spread to avoid doubt. So what is the spread of credit? It is essentially an options strategy to be developed with the same expiration month by either using put options or call options. "This approach is part of the family of "vertical spread."

If a trader is bullish on the underlying stock or index, at a higher strike, he/she may sell a put option and buy a put option at the same time at a lower strike with the same expiration month. Conversely, if a trader is bearish on the underlying stock or index at a lower strike, he/she may sell a call option and purchase a call option at the same time at a higher strike with same month of expiration.

Based on my coaching experience, the ideas of trading credit spreads fascinated quite a number of them because they seem to believe that their brokers would pay them for initiating new credit spreads. It sounds like "risk-free trades," doesn't it? This way is partly due to the word "credit," which indicates that a trader can receive free money from his/her brokers in the above context.

Sadly, this is not the case because there is no such thing called a credit spread in the options world known by market makers. There is no free lunch, and when initiating a new options position, no traders will be paid. In reality, if I were to use "credit spread," my mentors would scold me because the correct terminology for them is "selling a put spread." Suppose we are bullish on the underlying stock or index or "selling a call spread" if we are bearish on the underlying stock or index.

What's my point here? In reality, the answer is that a credit spread is a debit spread and a credit spread is a debit spread. No brokers will pay their customers to sell a call spread or a put spread (and that means other traders and me). The truth is that if it goes dead wrong, our brokers will charge us a margin that substantially represents the maximum risk of the spread.

Did you hear about the synthetic connection in the trading of options? You should, if not. It is possible to construct all "credit" put/call synthetically spreads as "debit" call/ put spreads because of the artificial relationship. Let us use a hypothetical stock - XYZ, currently trading at $360 per share, to go through the following example.

Suppose, on XYZ, we're bullish. A 355-350 put spread (i.e., selling 1 x 355 set and buying 1 x 350 put simultaneously) can be sold at, say, $0.60. In this case, the maximum trade reward is $0.60 with a $4.40 (i.e., $5.00 - $0.60) margin. Due to the synthetic relationship, by buying a 350-355 call spread (i.e., buying 1 x 350 call and simultaneously selling 1 x 355 call) for $ 4.40, we should create the same position, which means that the maximum reward will be $ 0.60.

CHAPTER 2 RULES FOR SUCCESSFUL TRADING

Ensuring dependable profits in the financial markets is much more difficult than it seems at first glance. It is assessed that over 75% of all members in the end wash out and take up more secure side interests. Be that as it may, the financier business once in a while distributes customer disappointment rates, since they're concerned reality may drive away new records, so the washout rate could be a lot higher.

The Road to Long-Term Profitability

Long haul benefit requires two interrelated ranges of abilities. To begin with, we need techniques that get more cash-flow than they lose. Second, those techniques must perform well while the market shape-moves through bull and bear driving forces, with a lot of uneven periods in the middle. While numerous brokers realize how to profit in explicit economic situations, similar to a solid upturn, they bomb over the long haul on the grounds that their techniques don't adjust to unavoidable changes.

So would you be able to split away from the pack and unite the expert minority with a methodology that raises your chances for long haul success? Begin with an unmistakable and succinct arrangement.

1.   Disregard the Holy Grail

Losing brokers fantasize about the mystery recipe that will mysteriously improve their outcomes. As a general rule, there are no mysteries in light of the fact that the way to progress consistently goes through cautious decision, viable risk the executives, and gifted benefit taking.

## 2.	Connect with Your Trading Plan

Update your trading plan week by week or month to month to incorporate new thoughts and kill awful ones. Return and read the arrangement at whatever point you fall in an opening and are searching for an approach to get out.

## 3.	Be careful with Reinforcement

Dynamic trading discharges adrenaline and endorphins. These synthetics can create sentiments of happiness notwithstanding when you are losing cash. Thus, this urges addictive characters to take terrible positions, just to get the hurry.

## 4.	Try not to Cut Corners

Your opposition burns through many hours consummating methodologies and you are in for a severe shock in the event that you hope to toss a couple of darts and leave with a benefit. It's far more terrible in the event that you cut corners in a mind-blowing remainder since that unfortunate propensity is a lot harder to break.

5. Grasp Simplicity

Concentrate on value activity, understanding that everything else is optional. Feel free to assemble complex specialized markers yet remember their essential capacity is to affirm or disprove what your prepared eye as of now observes.

6. Evade the Obvious

Benefit infrequently pursues the greater part. When you see an ideal exchange arrangement, almost certainly, every other person sees it too, planting you in the group and setting you up for disappointment.

7. Arrange Your Personal Life

Whatever is not right in your life will in the end persist into your trading execution. This is particularly risky on the off chance that you haven't profited, riches and the attractive extremity of plenitude and shortage.

8. Try not to Break Your Rules

You make trading principles to get you out of inconvenience when positions go seriously. On the off chance that you don't enable them to carry out their responsibility, you have lost your order and opened the entryway to significantly more noteworthy misfortunes.

9. Tune in to Your Intuition

Trading utilizes the scientific and imaginative sides of your cerebrum so you have to develop both to prevail over the long haul. When you are alright with math, you can upgrade results with reflection, a couple of yoga stances or a tranquil stroll in the recreation center.

10. Make Peace with Losses

Trading is one of only a handful couple of callings where losing cash each day is a characteristic way to progress. Each trading misfortune accompanies a significant market exercise in case you are available to the message.

11. Try not to Believe in a Company

In case you are excessively enamored with your trading vehicle, you offer approach to defective basic leadership. You must gain by wastefulness, profiting while every other person is inclining the incorrect way.

12.   Lose the Crowd

Long haul productivity requires situating in front of or behind the group, yet never in the group since that is the place savage techniques target. Avoid stock sheets and visit rooms. This is not kidding business and everybody in those spots has an ulterior thought process.

13.   Try not to Try to Get Even

Drawdowns are a characteristic piece of the merchant's life cycle. Acknowledge them effortlessly and adhere to the reliable methodologies you realize will in the long run recover your presentation on track.

14.   Try not to Count Your Chickens

Like an exchange that is going your direction yet the cash is not yours until you close out. Lock in what you can as ahead of schedule as possible, with trailing stops or fractional benefits, so concealed hands cannot pickpocket your prosperity ultimately.

15.   Watch for Early Warnings

Huge misfortunes once in a while happen without various specialized admonitions. Dealers routinely overlook those signs and enable would like to supplant keen control, setting themselves up for torment.

16.   Pursue Your Discipline

Order cannot be instructed in a workshop or found in costly trading programming. Dealers burn through a great many dollars attempting to make up for their absence of poise yet few understand that a long look in the mirror achieves a similar assignment at a lot less expensive cost!

17.   Apparatuses Don't Think

Dealers compensate for deficient aptitudes with costly programming, prepackaged with a wide range of exclusive purchase and sell signals. These apparatuses meddle with important experience since you think the product is more brilliant than you are.

18.   Play with Your Head

It's normal for dealers to copy their monetary saints but at the same time it's an ideal method to lose cash. Take in what you can from others, at that point back off and set up your very own market personality, in light of your one of a kind abilities and risk resistance.

19. Jettison the Paycheck Mentality

We're educated to pound through the stir week and afterward get our checks. This compensation for-exertion remunerate mindset clashes with the common progression of trading wins and misfortunes over the span of a year. Truth be told, insights show that most yearly benefits are set up for only a bunch of days the market is open for business.

20. Stay away from Market Gurus

It's your cash in question, not theirs. Remember that they're likely talking up their positions, trusting the energized prattle will expand their benefits, not yours.

Most by far of dealer's neglect to tap their maximum capacity, in the end trading in for cold hard currency their chips and discovering progressively customary approaches to profit. Become a pleased individual from the expert minority by following exemplary principles intended to keep a well-honed spotlight on productivity.

CHAPTER 3 MISTAKES TO AVOID IN OPTIONS TRADING

Trading options are more involved than trading stocks, so there are ample opportunities to make mistakes. It's important to take the approach of going small and slow at first so that you don't lose the shirt off your back. That said, if you run into mistakes, don't get too down about it. Dust yourself off and get up to fight another day. With that said, let's have a look at some common mistakes and how to avoid them.

Putting All Your Eggs in One Basket

While there is a difference between investing and trading, traders can learn a few things from our investor brothers (and most people are a little of both anyway). Don't let everything ride on one trade. If you take all the money you have and invest it in buying options for one stock, you're making a big mistake. Doing that is very risky, and as a beginning trader, you're going to want to mitigate your risk as much as possible. Betting on one stock may pay off sometimes, but more times than not it's going to lead you into bankruptcy territory.

Investing More than You Can

It's easy to get excited about options trading. The chances to make fast money and the requirements that you analyze the markets can be very enticing. Oftentimes that leads people into getting more excited than they should. A good rule to follow with investing is to make sure that you're setting aside enough money to cover living expenses every month, with a security fund for emergencies. Don't bet the farm on some sure thing by convincing yourself that you'll be able to make back twice as much money and so cover your expenses. Things don't always work out.

Going All in Before You're Ready

Another mistake is failing to take the time to learn options trading in real time. Just like getting overly excited can cause people to bet too much money or put all their money on one stock, some people are impatient and don't want to take the time to learn the options markets by selling covered calls. It's best to start with covered calls and then move slowly to small deals buying call options. Leave put options until you've gained some experience.

Failure to Study the Markets

Remember, you need to be truly educated to make good options trades. That means you'll need to know a lot about the companies that you're either trying to profit from or that you're shorting. Options trading isn't possible without some level of guesswork, but make your guesses, educated guesses, and don't rely too much on hunches.

Not Getting Enough Time Value

Oftentimes, whether you're trading puts or calls, the time value is important. A stock may need an adequate window of time in order to beat the stock price, whether it's going above it or plunging below it. When you're starting out and don't know the markets as well as a seasoned trader, you should stick to options you can buy that have a longer time period before expiring.

Not Having Adequate Liquidity

Sometimes beginning investors overestimate their ability to play the options markets. Remember that if you buy an option, to make it work for you—you're going to need money on hand to buy stocks when the iron is hot. And you're going to need to buy 100 shares for every option contract.

Not Having a Grip on Volatility

If you don't understand volatility and its relation to premium pricing, you may end up making bad trades.

Failing to Have a Plan

Trading seems exciting, and when you're trading, you may lose the investors' mentality. However, traders need to have a strategic plan as much as investors do. Before trading, make sure that you have everything in place, including knowing what your goals are for the trades, having pre-planned exit strategies, developing criteria for getting into a trade so that you're not doing on a whim or based on emotion.

Ignoring Expiration Dates

It sounds crazy, but many beginners don't keep track of the expiration date. Would you hate to see a stock go up in price, and then hope it keeps going up, and it does, only to find out that your expiration date passed before you exercised your option?

Overleveraging

It's easy to spend huge amounts of money in small increments. This is true when it comes to trading options. Since stocks are more expensive, it's possible to get seduced by purchasing low priced options. After all, options are available at a fraction of the cost that is required to buy stocks. And you might keep on purchasing them until you're overleveraged.

Buying Cheap Options

In many cases, buying cheap things, isn't a good strategy. If you're buying a used car, while you might occasionally find a great car that is a good buy, in most cases, a car is cheap for a reason. The same applies to options trading. When it comes to options, a cheap premium probably denotes the option is out of the money. Sure, you save some money on a cheap premium, but when the expiration date comes, you might see the real reason the option contract was a cheap buy. Of course, as we described earlier, there may be cases where cheaper options have the capacity to rebound and become profitable by the time the expiry date arrives. But taking chances like that is best left to experienced traders.

Giving in to Panic

Some beginners panic and exercise their right far too early. This can happen because of fears that they'll be missing out an opportunity with a call option, or because of fears that a stock won't keep going down on a put.

Going into options trading blindly is not a smart move. With each option trade you make, you need to have a clear idea of how much cash you have on hand to cover losses and exercising your options. You'll also want to know how much cash you can afford to lose if things go south.

Jumping into Puts Without Enough Experience and Cash to Cover Losses

Remember, if you're selling puts, you will have to buy the stock at the strike price if the buyer exercises their option. This is a huge risk. The stock could have plunged in value, and you're going to have to buy the stock at the strike price, possibly leaving you with huge losses. Don't go into selling puts with your eyes closed, in fact, beginners are better off avoiding selling puts. But if you must do it, make sure you can absorb the losses when you bet wrong.

Piling It On

Most beginner mistakes are related to panic. If you're looking at losses on options, some beginners double and triple up, hoping to make it up when things turn better. Instead, they end up losing more money. Instead of giving in to panic, learn when to cut your losses and re-evaluate your trading strategy.

Staying in a Written Contract When You Should Get Out

If you've sold an option and it's looking like you might face a loss, you can always get out of it by selling.

CHAPTER 4 ANALYZING MARKET TRENDS IN OPTIONS TRADING

Nearly every option trader has heard the old trade adage that says, "The trend is your buddy." In reality, an option trading against the current market trend certainly puts the odds of winning for you. So many newcomers have lost whole accounts through the purchasing of call options from the bear trend market and the purchasing of options from the bull trend market.

Yeah, what is a business phenomenon exactly?

Similarly, you know it's a bullish phenomenon when you see the bigger and higher indexes like the Dow Jones Industrial Average or the S&P500, and you realize it's a weird phenomenon when you see the smaller and lower indexes.

Yeah, market patterns are general movements that tend to shift stocks. During a bull market, the prices of most stocks will rise and grow, and the prices of most stocks will decline and drop.

One thing about trends is, however, that trends are a "general course of movement". It does not mean that a bull trend just drives the market up every day and does not mean that a bear trend just drives the market down.

When you watch the ocean tides, the water does not rush on the beach in a rising tide but falls in the waves. One wave is stronger than the last. The same is true of stock market patterns. You will see days interspersed with days in a bull cycle. However, notifications will occur more regularly and will every after each slight retreat.

Traders who fall for either trap are usually shocked when the general trend resumes and are stuck in a losing position which never turns around.

Recognizing how patterns work is just the first step to business patterns identification. Have you ever believed that the economy is just one way to disagree with it by peers? How can two people who look at the same market draw different conclusions about the trend in the market?

The challenge of understanding consumer patterns is that the demand can be in all three directions at any point on the same day!

The market might be in a downturn for day traders, but on the same day, it could be in a bull downturn for a day trader and a long-term investor's neutral pattern. How can that be?

In reality, there are not just "business" conditions; depending on the timeframe, there are multiple market conditions! It is not known that there is a common consumer trend for various trade horizons and investment targets, which contributed to all the pointless debates about what the business trend is in television.

A diagram that looks incredibly strange in the 1-minute table might look extremely stable and chaotic on a regular map. As such, trend analysis includes in the first place an appreciation of the exact time frame in which you trade.

Acknowledgment of the exact time you are trading is an extremely important precondition for options trading, where the contracts and positions you have bought are time-sensitive! Yeah, options do not last forever, and all choice approaches have an optimized return period.

For example, the market trend you would be concerned with will be the intraday trend most widely associated with minute charts, whether you are trading on the day with options and either writing or purchasing the options to close them for profit by the end of the trading day.

In this situation, whether the market is in a long-term bull or bear trend no longer affects your trading. The world may be crying, but if your minute charts show bearish for the day, the way you make your money is bearish.

If you trade a covered call, you will want to write the call options on a stock that is fairly lateral to the market trading charts in the regular charts if you want to prevent the allocation of stocks.

In comparison, if you buy long-term LEAPS options, you may be more interested in what the long-term market trend is instead of being too concerned with uncertainty every day.

So, what are the most important methods for identifying business trends?

Most veterans can identify the pattern in which a map looks much like a price chart. However, countless complex technological metrics have been developed over the years for the less skilled or technically inclined.

Personally, the Simple Moving Average is the most tested. That simply averages the price over a period of time to see where it normally goes. This is what I focus on most of the time personally and I use a different average period for different time horizons. The 30days or 50days are most widely used.

CHAPTER 5 RECOGNIZING TRADING OPPORTUNITIES

A key piece of alternatives exchanging is centers around discovering chances to make exchanges. There are various ways that you can recognize and survey such chances, and we have given data on what is engaged with the procedure. To be effective in your exchanging, you will have a lot of chances for exchanges, so this is unquestionably something you should submit some an opportunity to.

On the off chance that you have been perusing this guide so as to assist you with beginning with alternatives exchanging, you will thoroughly understand the underlying readiness required and how to pick a merchant. You'll additionally have a comprehension of exchanging levels and how they can influence your capacity to utilize certain procedures.

At this stage it's an ideal opportunity to begin pondering how you are going to discover chances to exchange. You could know totally everything there is to think about choices exchanging, however such information is just valuable in the event that you can really try everything and recognize chances to make a few benefits.

Despite the fact that alternatives exchanging is actually very perplexing, anybody that is set up to invest energy learning the subject can eventually be effective. Be that as it may, realizing how to exchange alternatives isn't sufficient without anyone else; you have to realize how to bring in cash out of it. This takes difficult work and responsibility since; you should invest the necessary exertion so as to locate the correct chances and afterward make the proper exchanges.

In the event that you can do that reliably, at that point you will very likely accomplish your objectives. On this page we take a gander at how you approach distinguishing possibly beneficial open doors for exchanging choices.

1. Which Underlying Assets?

Despite the fact that choices contracts are resources themselves, they are really subordinating that get their incentive from the hidden resources which they identify with. Choices agreements can be purchased and sold on a wide scope of basic resources that incorporate stocks, remote monetary forms, wares, and lists.

This makes choices exchanging a truly adaptable type of contributing in light of the fact that, you can make speculations on a wide range of monetary instruments just by purchasing and selling choices contracts. This implies one of the principal things you have to consider whenever you are searching for potential choices exchanging openings is actually which of these money related instruments you need to incorporate.

We ought to be evident that you don't have to choose to exchange just investment opportunities, or just forex choices, or just file alternatives. You can purchase and sell the same number of various sorts of choices as you feel great with. Be that as it may, you do need to consider how you will be examining potential exchanges and how you'll be recognizing appropriate chances.

On the off chance that you concluded that you would think about a wide range of various hidden protections, at that point you would be giving yourself the most obvious opportunity with regards to discovering openings due to the wide scope of conceivable outcomes. You would should be readied, however, to complete a great deal of investigation into various money related markets which could be very tedious and it could really make it exceptionally hard to locate the quantity of chances as you might want.

On the other hand, on the off chance that you concluded that you were just going to exchange investment opportunities dependent on stocks in a specific division, at that point you would have the option to concentrate your examination explicitly on publically recorded organizations that work around there. You may wind up turning into a specialist in that field and be significantly more adroit at distinguishing related open doors dependent on this skill.

The drawback, obviously, to adopting such a restricted strategy is, that you might be passing up loads of different open doors in various segments and markets that you aren't in any event, taking a gander at.

There truly is no correct way, or incorrect way, to move toward this part of distinguishing openings and we wouldn't offer a particular guidance in such manner. All we would recommend is that you set aside the effort to consider which fundamental resources you need to incorporate and afterward it's eventually down to what you feel great with and what you think will give you the most obvious opportunity with regards to progress.

On the off chance that you do have solid information about a specific segment or market, at that point it would bode well to use that information, however there is likewise nothing amiss with taking a more extensive view either. You may conclude that you would prefer not to inquire about and investigate the fundamental resources of alternatives, yet would prefer to contemplate the value developments of the choices contracts themselves and exchange in like manner.

2. Doing Research

The coming of the plan and online innovation has influenced exchanging and interest in more than one way. Not just has it brought about online dealers, which make the entire procedure of purchasing and selling of monetary instruments a lot simpler, it has additionally made data identifying with money related instruments significantly more open.

The web gives a for all intents and purposes boundless flexibly of data that can be utilized for look into purposes, and this truly is significant to financial specialists. It's fundamental to begin checking the trades to get modern statements and to follow universal news that can influence the business sectors. In any event, getting money related reports on publically recorded organizations is something essential to do. The web is a rich wellspring of realities, measurements, and figures that can help gigantically.

Obviously, gathering data is just a single piece of doing research for exchanging purposes. The genuine aptitude is in comprehending what data to search for and afterward realizing how to decipher it. This is an ability in itself, yet it's an expertise that can be effortlessly evolved after some time with a lot of training.

In the event that you are set up to commit a not too bad measure of time to doing research and breaking down what you discover then you truly will give yourself a greatly improved possibility of progress with regards to finding conceivably beneficial chances.

3. Central and Technical Analysis

Central investigation and specialized examination are the two principle strategies utilized by speculators and brokers to break down data and help figure out what exchanges and ventures to make. In spite of the fact that they are both basically utilized for a similar reason, they are altogether different in the manner in which they are utilized.

Essential examination is fundamentally about gathering however much data as could reasonably be expected identifying with a particular security and afterward dissecting that data to decide the genuine estimation of that security and how it identifies with its exchanging cost.

For instance, on the off chance that you need to do central investigation on a stock in a specific organization, at that point you would consider various parts of that organization, for example, their current money related quality, their profit reports, the nature of their administration work force, and their serious edge in the commercial center. By doing this, you could get a thought of whether the stock was underestimated, exaggerated, or estimated directly comparable to its actual worth. This is to some degree improved, yet it gives you a thought of how essential investigation is utilized.

Specialized investigation is based around utilizing past information to foresee future developments. It includes considering and dissecting outlines and diagrams delineating cost and volume, with the end goal of discovering designs that could uncover patterns that are probably going to be rehashed. The hypothesis is that by following those patterns you can make precise estimates about how a security is going to move in cost over a given period time. Once more, this is a genuinely streamlined perspective on specialized examination, yet it's a sensible outline of what is included.

Both basic examination and specialized investigation are commonly utilized by speculators in stocks, however they have their utilization in alternatives exchanging as well. The general thought is that you would utilize these strategies to assist you with getting a thought of how you would anticipate that the cost of money related instruments should move, and afterward exchange the fitting alternatives agreements to profit by those moves.

Neither principal investigation nor specialized examination can truly be viewed as better than the other one as there are various variables to consider. Somewhat it boils down to individual inclination; in the event that you feel increasingly good utilizing one of the procedures for your examination, or have a specific fitness for it, at that point it clearly bodes well to utilize that strategy. You may like to utilize a mix of both, or utilize key investigation in certain conditions and specialized examination in others.

It merits nothing, however, that choices exchanging is frequently about exploiting transient value developments as opposed to whatever else. Crucial examination can assist you with increasing a comprehension of the innate worth of a security, and it is usually utilized by long haul financial specialists to put resources into underestimated stocks that ought to go up in cost after some time. Be that as it may, it doesn't really assist you with foreseeing value developments in the prompt term.

Specialized examination can, which is the reason choices dealers are most likely bound to profit by utilizing specialized investigation: especially those utilizing a day exchanging style and making a few transient exchanges regularly.

Something else to consider when you are recognizing potential exchanges is how much capital is required and how much hazard is included. Dealing with your spending plan and your introduction to hazard is a significant piece of alternatives exchanging.

Hazard and Money Management

Great administration of your introduction to chance and your exchanging capital is totally crucial in any type of exchanging on the off chance that you can bring in cash over the long haul.

Effectively dealing with your capital and hazard introduction is basic when exchanging choices. While chance is basically unavoidable with any type of venture, your introduction to chance doesn't need to be an issue. The key is to deal with the hazard reserves viably; consistently guarantee that you are OK with the degree of hazard being taken and that you aren't presenting yourself to unreasonable misfortunes.

CHAPTER 6 DAILY ROUTINE FOR A TRADER

Missteps occur in options trading. They regularly happen on the grounds that an excessive amount of data is coming in without a moment's delay and you feel over-burden, froze, and forceful, or they frequently happen during calm/bring times when your watchman is down. Furthermore, obviously, there are constantly irregular mix-ups, for example, hitting an inappropriate catch – purchase rather than sell – or putting out an inappropriate position size. Such blunders can even occur with robotized methodologies.

Before each trading day take a couple of minutes to experience multi day trading routine to help limit mistakes for the duration of the day. Here are the means to experience. Contingent upon the market you exchange, you may wish to include a couple of extra advances. This entire procedure just takes a few minutes however spares you a great deal of dissatisfaction and cash.

1 Conditions in the Market

Make a brisk appraisal of trading conditions up until now. Is the pre-advertise demonstrating a great deal of instability, or is it steady? Is there a pattern or explicit propensities you take note?

Such an evaluation tells you how to continue, and whether you ought to exchange your framework by any stretch of the imagination. This is particularly significant if utilizing an emotional framework – a framework that fluctuates marginally dependent on economic situations. For instance, in unpredictable conditions, you may have a bigger expected benefit focus than on multi day when there is no unpredictability.

2 Keep Notes

On your graph, put content notes expressing when high effect news discharges are. Whenever fascinated in an exchange you may disregard one of these occasions, and it could cost you beyond all doubt. Record it on your diagram. In the event that the occasion happens later in the day, look over and put the content note close to the estimated time of the declaration.

3 Launch Platform is Vital

Dispatch your stage. Ensure statements are gushing (not slacking or sporadic) and the program is running easily. Most intermediaries give dependable information encourages, yet issues can emerge. In the event that the information feed is irregular or appears to be erroneous, don't exchange until the issue is fixed. On the off chance that it looks right, continue.

4 Automated Strategies Should Be Confirmed

Regardless of whether your day exchange physically, you may have some robotized orders. For instance, in Ninja Trader and Meta Trader, you can convey stop misfortune requests and focuses on the minute you enter a position. Ensure these stop misfortune requests and targets are set properly. In the event that trading with a "robot," ensure all settings are exact before beginning it.

5 Have an End Time

In the event that you see a time you pattern to give back benefits all the time, compose a note to yourself to quit trading around then. In the event that you see this inclination, don't battle it. Quit trading during portions of the day you commonly lose cash. Help yourself to remember this when you start trading every day.

6 Have a Starting Position Size

In the event that you exchange with a default position size, ensure it is set fittingly. Adding an additional digit to a position size could spell catastrophe. Dropping a digit implies you exchange a small amount of what you could have, and you pass up a chance.

On the off chance that you physically change your position size dependent on your entrance point and stop misfortune areas, note your record balance before trading. Legitimate position measuring limits risk to a little level of record capital, for example, 2%. In the event that you have a $40,000 account, you can risk up to $400 on an exchange. Remember this greatest risk for the duration of the day (or compose a content note on your screen) to remind yourself this is the most you can risk on one exchange.

7 The Economic Calendar Must Be Considered

High effect monetary occasions can cause value spikes/holes, making critical slippage (the distinction between the value you expect and the value you get) on stop misfortune orders. It's ideal to abstain from being in exchanges for the couple of minutes encompassing high effect planned news occasion. Check your monetary schedule before trading, and note the high effect news times. For U.S. stocks and prospects, you can utilize Bloomberg. For Forex, look at the Daily FX financial schedule.

On the off chance that you exchange individual stocks all the time, check the organization does not have income or different declarations due out that day. The Yahoo! Finance profit schedule functions admirably. Know about these occasions, to abstain from trading directly before the declaration.

8 Important Thoughts

Help yourself to remember your risky propensities, and how you will deal with those circumstances should they emerge. Go over your Key Trading Thoughts.

9 Be Mindful as You Start Trading

You are set to exchange. This procedure should help dispense with certain errors identified with position size, trading an inappropriate record/contract, trading during news or just not setting up your brain to exchange.

As you begin searching for potential exchange arrangements, remember your Key Trading Thoughts. This will help keep you out of awful exchanges (ones not in your trading plan) and keep you caution and prepared to jump on great chances.

10 Use the Right Trading Account

In Meta Trader and Ninja Trader (for instance) you can sign in to various records utilizing a similar stage. Ensure you are trading the right record. You would prefer not to have an incredible day, just to acknowledge you traded in recreation rather than with genuine capital. In the event that day trading prospects, ensure you are trading the right most noteworthy volume contract. Know about termination dates on the agreements you exchange.

11 Make a Trading Routine

Your day trading routine may shift marginally from this, contingent upon your trading style and the market you exchange. Make a daily schedule however. It just takes about a moment or two to experience, and can spare you from a great deal of dissatisfaction.

CHAPTER 7   OPTIONS ON FUTURES

A future contract option gives the holder the right, but not the obligation, to purchase or sell a particular future contract at a strike price on or before the expiry date of the option. These work in the same way as stock options, but they differ because the underlying safety is a future agreement.

Many future options, such as index options, are settled in cash. These are also European-style options, meaning that these cannot be exercised early.

How Options On Futures Work

An option for a Future Contract is similar to that for a stock option in that it allows the buyer to buy or sell the underlying asset but not to have the obligation. This means the option for a futures contract or futures option is derivative security. But the price and contract characteristics of these options do not necessarily add to the leverage.

Therefore, an option for a future S&P 500 contract can be considered a second derivative of the S&P 500 index since its futures are derivatives of the index themselves. There are, therefore, more variables to be taken into account since the option and the futures contract have expiry dates and their own supply and demand profiles. Time decay (also known as theta), functions in the same way as options in other securities, and traders have to take this factor into consideration.

The buyer of the option will enter into the long part of the contract for the call options in the future and purchase the underlying asset at the strike price of the option. With options, the option holder will enter the brief side of the contract and sell the underlying asset at the price of the right.

Example of Options on Futures

For an example of how such contracts work, a potential S&P 500 contract will be considered first. E-mini S&P 500, is the most common S&P 500 contract and allows an investor to manage a cash amount worth 50 times the value of the S&P 500 Index. This e-mini contract will monitor the amount of $150,000 in cash should the index value be $3,000. If the index value rose by one percent to $3030, then the controlled cash would amount to $151,500. The difference here is an increase of $1,500. Because this future contract requires a margin of $6,300 (as of this letter), this change would mean a benefit of 25 percent.

But rather than raise $6,300 in cash, it would be considerably cheaper to buy an option on the index. For instance, if the index costs $3,000, suppose an option for the $3,010 strike price can also be quoted at $17,00 with two weeks in advance. A buyer of this option would not be required to maintain the $6,300 margin, but would only have to pay the price of the option. This is $50 times the cost (the same multiplier as the index) of every dollar spent.

This means that the option price is $850 plus commissions and fees, and around 85% less than the future contract.

Although this option moves with the same leverage ($50 per index $1), the cash leverage used may be considerably higher. If the index rises to $3030 in a single day, as stated in the example above, the option price could go from $17.00 to $32.00. This would mean an increase in the value of $750, which would not be the benefit on the futures contract alone, but would be an 88% increase instead of a 25% increase for the same amount of movements in the underlying index compared to the risks of 850$. Depending on the option to be purchased, the money traded can be leveraged or not to a greater extent than with the future alone.

Further Considerations for Options on Futures

As stated, when assessing an option on a futures contract, there are many moving parts to consider. Each of them is the fair value from the cash or the spot price of the underlying asset. The difference in the future contract is called a premium.

However, the options allow the owner, thanks to higher-margin rules (called the SPAN margin), to manage the large sums of the underlying asset with less capital. It offers additional leverage and revenues. But the profit potential leads to losses up to the full value of the contract options acquired.

The main difference between stock options and futures options is the variance in the underlying value of the stock option price. A $1 stock options change equals $1 (per share), which is uniform for all stocks. For each contract purchased, a $1 price change is worth $50 using the example of e-mini S&P 500 futures. This is not true for all futures and futures options markets. It is heavily dependent on the amount and the specifications of the goods, index, or bond defined in each future contract.

CHAPTER 8 DEMO
SIMULATOR & HOW TO USE
IT

Investing in the stock market, as the experts point out, requires substantial knowledge and experience to control the risk and make the appropriate decisions at the right time.

These simulators generally offer very advanced interfaces, a virtual economic fund to invest in, and real-time information. That is to say, they have all the tools and functions necessary to learn how to invest in an online stock market as if we were in the stock market itself.

Many of these computer programs belong to banks and brokers specialized in the stock market or markets such as Forex (such as Plus500). These applications, from our point of view, are more complete than the simple stock market games that we have found in the market for decades or than the apps that have overwhelmingly increased in recent years.

Most offer free demo accounts, although in some cases, we can find companies that request a small payment in exchange for using their platform. A small expense that is worth taking on and that can save us many dislikes in the future.

Why Use a Bag Simulator?

Investing in the stock market is not especially difficult, but it is essential to have good knowledge to avoid greater evils.

That is why it is essential to train previously in everything related to the markets and their operation. For this, you can go to the editorial fund of the National Commission of the Stock Market or the Madrid Stock Exchange, where we can find practical guides and handy tips for beginners and more advanced investors.

Having the advice of an expert is also a guarantee, but if you prefer to take the road alone, we recommend that you settle the bases well before playing with real money. The risk, as we have repeated, is high if it is operated without the necessary knowledge. The stock market is not a lottery that can make you rich by investing a few euros, so you should know all the mechanisms of the market entirely to understand where and when to put your money.

In this learning process, a good stock market simulator plays an essential role. With these tools, you can play with fictitious money, see how your decisions affect your income statement, and, most importantly, create solid pillars to leap to the real world of investments.

Another advantage is that the companies that offer these simulators allow you to directly operate with real money from the same or similar platform, so you will already be familiar with the interface. In many cases, it is only necessary to convert your demo account into a real account and make an income, without changing the program.

Pay for a bag simulator?

Many people are wondering what the best free bag simulator for beginners is.

Creating a CFD bag simulator that offers guarantees entails a considerable programming expense and high operating costs. That is why some companies ask for a small subscription in exchange for their use that does not usually reach 10 euros per month. A minimum amount for a tool that tells you how to learn to invest in the stock market from home, and that allows you to practice with all the guarantees; it's worth it by any standards, of course.

Also, it is widespread that with that small fee, the user has access to manuals, tutorials, webinars, and other teaching materials to support the practical part with theoretical foundations. Investing in the stock market in the short term is not recommended, so all this material can be of high relevance to fix concepts.

The Best Bag Simulators

Once this preamble has been completed, we will analyze five of the most exciting simulators in the market. All are backed by companies with ample experience in the sector (they are banks or brokers) and are well above in quality and performance of simple stock games (we do not recommend using these games as part of your training). This listing is sorted alphabetically.

Active Trade

This real-time stock market simulator offers users an account with 100,000 virtual euros so they can practice without fear of losing their money. It has personalized support and, most importantly, courses and trading programs taught by professional traders.

With this tool, you can create your strategy, control your investments, find the companies that best fit your profile, and get detailed information on more than 18,400 shares. Essential functions to create your profile as an investor and locate those opportunities that you can take advantage of in the real world.

IG Spain

The demo account of this stock market simulator allows you to invest in an online stock market in a risk-free environment. This free account has a virtual fund of 20,000 euros and offers graphics and prices in real-time. Also, you can check from your mobile or tablet to continue operating anywhere, even if you don't have a computer. The interface can be customized to suit your tastes and your style.

This demo account, however, does not offer all the functionality of the real platform. The most notable differences are the following:

• Transactions made through the demo account are not subject to slippage, interest or dividend adjustments, or price movements out of the negotiation.

• Transactions can be rejected if you do not have enough funds to open them, but they will not be denied due to size or price issues.

• The graphics packages have no cost.

• The positions will not be closed if you do not have enough funds to cover the margin or current losses, something that does happen in a real account.

Ore trade

Another easy-to-use bag simulator is that of Ore trade. With this tool, you will learn to invest in both the Spanish selective, that is, in the IBEX 35, as in other critical global exchanges. All online and free, since you can try it without cost and obligation.

Through its interface, you can access stock quotes in real-time and different analyses, comparative, and graphical tools. The account begins with a virtual fund of 100,000 euros to start investing.

Society General

This trading simulator seems to us one of the most interesting since it will allow you to delve into the world of warrants, something that is not available in most of the free tools. The simulator of this French bank makes available to its users 10,000 fictitious euros to negotiate on the listed products of Society General and test their investment strategy without risk.

To start operating, you must register on the website www.sgbolsa.es. Registration is free. Also, the entity usually raffles gifts such as mobile phones or tablets among its new users, one more argument to try the Market Simulator, as they call it.

Trader Twit

The Trader twit simulator catches our attention since it has enormous educational value. It is not free (although it is cheap), but instead offers training and a compelling platform. They have a lot of news from the sector, an exciting collaborative platform, and thousands of interactive analyses.

We like what they call "the challenge." It is something like a 50-level training program that puts users in challenges to move from level to level. In each of them, you have to follow instructions, such as the maximum lever that can be used or the maximum loss streak. There are also objectives to be achieved.

Based on these criteria, the user can carry out operations of buying and selling currencies, indices, or raw materials — an excellent way to learn while having fun and competing against other users in the community. Also, the best usually takes real prizes.

CHAPTER 9 WHEN TO ENTER AND EXIT THE TRADE

When you were a kid, did you ever play double Dutch jump rope? Double Dutch is where two people are swinging two lines, and a third person has to jump in for a bit before jumping out. As a kid, it was brutal and painful to find the right timing to jump in without getting hit with a rope. Entering into a trade can be just as nerve-wracking. You can be set up to join the business and stress yourself with questions like, "Do I jump in now? How about now?" But with some strategic planning and practice, you can find the best area you would like to jump in regularly.

The entry point in a trade is the point at which you want to buy an asset. It's the starting bid in your business. Whether you are trading stocks or options, you will always have to have an entry point. Having a good plan for when you will enter into a trade is beneficial because it means that you won't have to drive yourself mad. It also means that you won't be making an emotional choice regarding when to enter.

Choosing a good entry point means analyzing the chart for support, resistance, and trend. Look at the past movement of the table and find the support and resistance. Then, look at the direction. Has the chart been moving in a specific trend line? Or has it been in a stage of consolidation? Or a period where the market has remained relatively steady? With a stock that has a trend line, you can choose a point right after a rebound. For example, let's say stock ABC was trading at $60 in November before dropping to $58. As the number starts to rise again, you can see if the chart seems like it's going to return to trend. If yes, then you can place your entry point at $60 and wait to see if the trend will continue upward.

In the case of a stock that is at a stage \of the neutral movement, then your support and resistance lines will be horizontal, and the chart will remain between those two lines. In this case, follow the pattern of the movement and again place your entry point at the price where a rebound is likely to happen. This should be close to the support line. There's a good chance that the stock value will rise again towards the resistance in this case.

Let's put this into action.

Chose two different practice charts. One should have a stock that is trending upwards, and one should have stock that is steady and isn't trending in a particular direction. Taking the one that is trending upward, draw the trend line in the support line position. From there, choose a location that offers you a small swing up. At what point would you enter the swing? At what price point? How long would you remain in the swing? Do the same for the chart that is remaining steady. What location above the support line would you enter into the trade? It's easy to do this with past maps because everything is already lined up. But take the time to analyze the chart. What makes specific swings more successful, and what makes them unsuccessful?

Now try with a future practice trade. Again, find a chart from a stock that you would be interested in purchasing. Map out your lines, find the zone you'll trade-in, and then choose an entry point either in the present or the future. After that, watch the stock for the several days. Would your trade have panned out? If yes, why? And if no, why not? All of this practice allows you to try out deals before investing any capital into it. Once you feel a bit more confident about entry points, move on to learn about exit points.

When you enter into the trade, you need to make sure that your risk/reward ratio makes the deal worth it. Once you calculate the rate, you can determine at what point you can exit the trade to make the reward worth it.

Now we're going to learn how to exit a trade. It is essential to have an exit strategy. Without an exit strategy, you will choose to leave a business whenever you feel like it, which can cause you some losses. You may exit too early or too late. It is better to have a strategy in place so that you know exactly when you'll exit. For example, if you determine that you would like to make a specific amount of profit, that's your exit point. Don't go past that.

As you throw it, momentum keeps it going higher but at a slower pace until it reaches its peak. At this point, energy is zero, and the ball falls back to your hands. In a swing trade, you want to exit the deal before the momentum reaches zero. Not at the peak, but before the summit. This is because most traders will be looking to sell at the height of the trade, which will cause a drop in the market—selling early before the estimated peak is a risk. It might mean that you lose out if the ball continues to go much higher than you anticipated. However, you will still have made again before any reversal happens and you can always buy back into the trend if you want to.

When looking at the charts for a stock, you should keep in mind your entry position and where you would like to exit. If the stock has stayed steady over the last bit of time and remains in its range, then looking at the support and resistance can give you a good idea of where to exit. If you entered near the support, then you can determine at what point you would like to exit. This depends on a lot of factors like your tolerance for risk and how long you want to stay in the trade. Generally speaking, if the stock value keeps increasing, you want to exit before it hits the resistance. Remember, in swing trading; it's all about small gains, not large ones, so it's better to leave with some profit rather than no profit.

With your support and resistance marked on a chart, you can also look for key indicators that show you that it's time to sell. One of these indicators is either if the stock value exceeds its resistance, or if it drops below its support numbers. This can mean that it's starting to trend in one specific direction, but it could also mean that these little breakouts will backtrack into it was sitting at before. If the stock value exceeds its resistance and you haven't sold yet, then you can choose to wait until it returns to its range, or see if it will be the start of a new trend. This decision, again, depends on how much risk you're willing to take.

There are a couple of things you can do to make sure that you are not staying in a trade too long. The first one is to set a stop-loss. A stop-loss is a tool that will sell your shares if the stock price goes too low. The other option is to place a limit order. A limit order will sell your trades once they've reached your set peak value. Let's say that the current stock price for ABC is $20 per share when you enter. You can choose to place your limit order at $25 a share. You can also set it at a certain percentage point for profit. This means that at the $25 mark, your broker will sell your shares. This can be good because it can limit your losses, but it can also prevent you from taking advantage of a possible trend. So once again, make a decision based on your tolerance for risk.

As you make your exit strategy, you should ask yourself a few questions. You should know how long you are willing to stay in a trade, how much risk you can tolerate and at what point you want to get out. These three things will help you make a good exit strategy. For example, when asking yourself how long you want to stay in a trade, you can think about how long you want your capital to be tied up, what indicators you're looking for that will cause you to sell, etc.

When considering how much risk you're willing to take, try a few different scenarios. Also, think what a profit is to you. Is it a $1 per share a decent profit, or do you want to make more? Finally, consider when you want to leave the trade. You should have this written down clearly. Are you going to leave the business once you've made a guaranteed profit, once you hit the resistance level, or once you see another indication that it's time to go? When you've made your plan, you must stick to it. This will help you remain emotionally objective when trading.

Once you've made your exit plan, it's time again to practice. Look at some past charts and analyze where you would have entered and exited the trade, based on the indicators like support and resistance, or based on the moving average. Analyze every piece of a move. Why would a specific exit point have worked or failed? Afterwards, try this again with a future chart. You can either do this in a simulation or using your chart website of choice. Pick a stock you want to follow and find an entry point you think will work for you. Then, using your exit strategy, determine when you will exit the chart. Spend a few days looking at your plan as the table moves forward. Did your plan work? Are there other ways you could have executed it? Keep practicing, don't just do this with one chart and think you're ready to start trading.

CHAPTER 10 TIPS AND TRICKS

If you are interested in embarking on the journey of earning money through options trading, there are a few issues to address before getting on board. Here are some of them:

Know When to Go Off the Manuscript

While sticking to your plan, even when your emotions are telling you to ignore it, is the mark of a successful trader, this in no way means that you must blindly follow your plan 100 percent of the time. Without a doubt, you would get yourself in a situation from time to time where your plan is going to be rendered completely useless by something outside of your control. You must be mindful enough of your plan's weaknesses, as well as changing market conditions, to know when following your predetermined course of action is going to lead to failure instead of success. Knowing when the situation is changing versus when your emotions are trying to hold sway comes with practice, but even being aware of the disparity is a huge step in the right direction.

Avoid Trades That Are Out of the Money

While there are a few strategies out there that make it a point of picking up options that are currently out of the money, you can rest assured that they are most certainly the exception, not the rule. Remember, the options market is not like the traditional stock market, which means that even if you are trading options based on underlying stocks buying low and selling high is just not a viable strategy. If a call has dropped out of the money, there is generally less than a 10 percent chance that it will return to acceptable levels before it expires, which means that if you purchase these types of options, what you are doing is little better than gambling, and you can find ways to gamble with odds in your favor of much higher than 10 percent.

Never Get Started Without a Clear Plan for Entry and Exit

More important than setting entry and exit points, however, is using them, even when there is still the appearance of money on the table. One of the biggest hurdles that new options traders need to get over is the idea that you must squeeze every last cent out of every successful trade. The fact of the matter is that, as long as you have a profitable trading plan, then there will always be more profitable trades in the future, which means that instead of worrying about a small extra profit, you should be more concerned with protecting the profit that the trade has already netted you. While you may occasionally make some extra profit ignoring this advice, odds are you will lose far more than you gain as profits peak unexpectedly and begin dropping again before you can effectively pull the trigger.

Read

Read at least one manuscript per week. This technique will teach you a lot of things, especially secrets. It will also provide you with a deeper understanding of the risks and rewards involved.

Trade for Income Not Wealth

If you do this thinking that you will be getting returns at 120%, you should reconsider. While one or two investments may yield such returns, the vast majority of options will not.

Start with Enough Capital

The first things you need to make sure you are set up with includes having ample money to assist you get into the investment. Capital is the amount of money you can bring into your account to help pay for all of the transactions you choose, and if you end up taking a loss when trading, it can be used.

You should always leave a little bit of money in your trading account. This is going to help you out when you are in the middle of a trade and can make it easier for your broker to keep working on trades without having to worry about a delay while your fund's transfer.

Avoid the Really Big Risks

Good options traders don't like a ton of risk, and they don't understand why they should take a big gamble just so they can get a tiny chance at a big payday. Rather than going after things like this, they are going to work on some trades that are high gain but lower in risk.

Be Sure to Diversify

Diversification is of the utmost importance. Having a portfolio that is not adequately diversified is a rookie mistake; however, many professional investors prefer not to diversify because of the way money is run in the United States.

Try Not to Panic

People don't make money from panicking in stressful situations. You will always encounter better times to leave or make a move rather than moves brought about by nervousness or panic. This is the downfall of a lot of people who are interested in investing but can't seem to master the craft.

See the Positive About It and Find Opportunities

The following time you notice there is a situation with trading that has brought a lot of panic on, you should immediately take the opposing side. Some of the best trades you can make involve the trade having been cleared out from people panicking and using their market orders, without understanding that the doors for exiting are not as large as they believe or assume.

This doesn't mean all of the merchandise that people leave out of panic is worth investing in over long periods. Usually, when the market or stocks get socked, there will be a bounce-back that lets you leave in a better position than you would have if you went along with what everyone else was doing when they left too fast.

Trade at the Right Times

Since you are going to learn how to avoid big risks when you are an options trader, you are going to learn how to be very careful about your timing when it comes to entering and exiting the market. You should have the ability to analyze the market the right way so that you can learn the best time to do both of those tasks. These investors have spent their time doing some research, and they know how to look at the big picture, rather than always calling up the broker and hoping that they can trust that person.

Learn How to Be Focused

There are a few individuals who think that trading options is super easy, and then they jump in and get frustrated by what they are dealing with. If you are not used to this kind of investment, it may seem a bit hard to deal with in the beginning.

If you find that you are a person who is not able to easily focus on the task that you need to, then it is easy to have trouble with options trading because you are missing out on things. A trader who can maintain their focus for a long time is more likely to get more out of this trading style.

Never Follow the Crowd

One of the bad habits that you can do is try to follow the crowd and hope that will work out well for you. Many beginners find it easy to look to the experts for advice, and then they will follow exactly what that expert says without doing any of their research or trusting their judgment. There is nothing wrong with having an expert's advice, but your plan is not going to be the same as theirs. You are the only one who has an idea of your limits and your goals, and while you can listen to the advice that others give you, it is important to think for yourself and pick out a plan that works for you.

Keep It as Simple as Possible

Options trading is a complicated market by definition. You do not need to perplex things any further. Keep your strategies as simple as possible, use the simplest technical analysis tools, and manage your money in the simplest way possible. The rest will fall in place on their own.

Do Not Overtrade

When you start dealing with inexpensive options, it will be very easy to lose track of what you are trading with. Keep the number of contracts at a manageable level.

Pay Attention to Rankings

Especially if you are dealing with spreads, and particularly if you are a novice. Qualification rankings are available to consult at all times. An option that is not ranked high is not a good option and it will probably cost you money.

Be Consistent

You would want to have a good understanding of the pros and cons of the different stocks in question before you ever make any trade, as well as the best point to enter a trade and at which point you would want to leave the trade if things go badly, and also where you can exit if things actually go as well as you might expect. Once you have made a plan, it is important to stick with it even if your emotions are making a compelling argument for going in another direction instead. It is important to always trust in your plan as it was made during a period when you were thinking as rationally as possible; giving in to your emotions at this point is akin to gambling with your investments.

Keep the Mood of the Market in Mind at All Times

Fundamental and technical analysis is all well and good, but they will only take you so far before you run into instances where the market seems to balk at the logical choice and move off in an unexpected direction. This typically happens when the will of the market goes against the status quo thanks to an unexpected outpouring of support from traders who are thinking with their guts instead of their brains. The greatest way to go about doing this is to keep tabs on what the major players in your market of choice are up to, as this will typically act as a litmus test when it comes to the feelings of the market as a whole.

CONCLUSION

As you have been able to read in this book, there are no magic formulas to invest safely and earn money without any risk. There are, however, the correct techniques and some tricks that allow the careful and well-focused trader to get the most out of his investment strategies.

We hope that we have provided you with the knowledge to help you make a difference, but if you feel that you still need to learn more, if you want to learn the basic concepts of Options Trading or find the best investment strategies, we recommend reading the other books in the series:

OPTIONS TRADING CRASH COURSE: FUNDAMENTALS *Everything you need to know before you start investing like a real trader*

OPTIONS TRADING CRASH COURSE: INVESTING FOR BEGINNERS *Learn how to operate in the market in the best way even if you are just a beginner*

OPTIONS TRADING CRASH COURSE: SWING TRADING DAY TRADING AND BEST STRATEGIES *The best strategies to operate in the market in the most profitable way*

www.ingramcontent.com/pod-product-compliance
Lightning Source LLC
Chambersburg PA
CBHW060243230326

41458CB00094B/1415

* 9 7 8 1 9 1 4 5 9 9 7 6 7 *